BYPASS PILGRIM

BYPASS PILGRIM

Writings from
the Vicinity
of the Heart

Roy Bayfield

for Ailsa

~trans_genre_*books*

29 9 10

For Jennie

Six patients were interviewed and the key themes to emerge were fear/anxiety and uncertainty, with other themes being hope and acceptance of the need for the operation, frustration at the waiting, avoidance (of information related to their health), confusion (as to what was happening), shock and guilt (that they were to blame for their condition).

Patient education around cardiac surgery, Helen Goodman, British Journal of Cardiac Nursing 4(10): 483 - 488 (Oct 2009)

So Roy said good-bye to all her friends except Jennie, and taking the dog in her arms followed the green girl through seven passages and up three flights of stairs until they came to a room at the front of the Palace... Beautiful green flowers stood in the windows, and there was a shelf with a row of little green books. When Roy had time to open these books she found them full of queer green pictures that made her laugh, they were so funny.

'Personalised Classics' version of The Wonderful Wizard of Oz, L. Frank Baum and P. and J. Woodward-Wright, Gift Republic (2009)

Walk 8 times to the Green heart.

Information for Patients & Carers: Cardiac Surgery, Liverpool Heart and Chest Hospital NHS Trust (January 2008) Version 2 CTPALS064

Contents

Introduction

I had some mild physical discomfort
which turned out to be caused by hardened arteries, properly known as atherosclerosis. The treatment involved a coronary artery bypass graft operation. These pieces were written before and after this procedure which I had at Easter, 2010.

At the start of the year I had gone to my GP complaining of a pain in my shoulder experienced when walking in cold weather. I took some tests, and the cause was diagnosed as angina. I had walked through a one-way door and become a cardiac patient. In the place I found myself, I had to get used to the idea that blocked arteries were preventing my heart from getting sufficient oxygen. I was issued with drugs, including statins, beta-blockers and a 'nitro spray' which turned out to contain actual nitroglycerine, and which caused me to faint the second time I used it.

A week later a procedure called an angiogram revealed that a bypass was required to resolve the problem, which felt like the most drastic of the treatment options available. The operation would involve making better routes for the heart's blood and the oxygen it carries, using vessels taken from elsewhere in the body. The sternum would be cracked open for the surgeon to get access and incisions made in arms and/or legs to harvest veins with which to construct the bypasses. Recovery was expected to take two to three months. In an otherwise upbeat booklet from the British Heart Foundation I read that 'about 20 in every 1,000 people die in hospital after having coronary artery bypass surgery for the first time' (Heart Information Series Number 10, August 2004). Set against that statistic I was told that, if I did not have the bypass, there would be a one-in-four chance of having a heart attack within a year. Consenting to the surgery was an easy decision to make.

Waiting for this major operation to take place was an unsettled time that brought strange fears and unexpected joys. My wife Jennie and I suddenly had to reconfigure our lives around this 'bypass', preparing for my week in hospital and months of recovery. Meals were cooked and frozen, friends telephoned, tears shed, DVDs purchased, wills made. Contemplating a new and unimaginable covenant with my own body I started scribbling in notebooks while we moved from clinic to cinema to supermarket on a kind of fearful holiday.

The surgery was carried out at the excellent Liverpool Heart and Chest Hospital, colloquially known as Broadgreen. Five grafts were done in a five hour operation followed by five days on Ward E, an unsteady walk across wet grass in chilly sunshine to the car, and home—feeling fine, albeit wasted from the aftereffects of general anaesthetic, and bearing long scars on arm, leg and chest. It had worked; not, they say, a cure but rather a fix that should hold for a long time: the alarm cannot be turned off but the snooze button should work for decades. The whole process, staring with the GP visit, had taken less than 10 weeks. I have nothing but praise for the NHS staff and what they have done, and continue to do, for me.

During the subsequent months of rest, recovery and rehabilitation, while I began to feel better than I had before the operation, I worked on the earlier scribblings and wrote some more. And decided to set it all down in a book, doing some breaking open and slicing up of my own to make, as best I could, a gift, love-letter, apology, self-portrait, account, waystation on a journey towards writing other things, and escape plan.

Now submitted for your attention.

I have been walking home
between Southport and my hometown of Brighton, a few miles at a time, documenting the journey in a blog titled *Walking Home to 50*. The pieces on the following pages headed 'Walking Journal' started life in the blog, which can be seen in full at <walkinghometo50.wordpress.com>.

The bypass came as an interruption to, or perhaps a detour from, the combined processes of walking home and approaching my 50th birthday. I had got as far as Langley in Berkshire, never imagining that my journey would be stalled there for several months. For me the act of walking is profoundly linked with the whole heart-health-bypass package. Walking revealed the symptoms. Walking has been a key component of the recovery (starting with a journey across the floor of the ward the day after the operation, continuing with ever-lengthening walks in the hospital and at home). Walking links together the events and places that are important to me, which now include hospitals and clinics, consultations and procedures. This book is also, therefore, a kind of non-functioning guidebook, imaginary map and (should you so desire) object to leave by the wayside.

Ignore everything I write
particularly about treatment and medication, especially if you yourself have a cardiac condition. All such treatments are unique so my experience won't be the same as yours. In these pages I have explored fear and fragility, camped it up into a gothic pantomime and generally made a big deal out of it. Writing in this way was one of my side effects, harvesting words to build my own bypasses. If I were just *telling* you about it I would say that it was a routine, safe procedure—surprisingly pain-free—that has brought me immense benefits.

So don't worry. We'll be fine.

1: DIAGNOSIS

When the blood creeps, and the nerves prick
In Memoriam, Alfred, Lord Tennyson (1850)

I haven't done much walking recently, but I did manage to get a few hundred stationary metres in today at Southport Hospital, taking what is known as a 'treadmill test'. This is a bit like going on a stepping machine at a gym, but with wires stuck on one's chest, and lie-detector lines being drawn on screens and paper. I was advised not to look down, but instead to focus on the noticeboard filled with holiday postcards at eye-level in front of me—cheerful things, slightly faded, with a blue cast resulting from the endurance of cyan ink relative to other pigments. There was a girl in a thong on a Greek island, and a star-shaped promontory in St Petersburg... While I rested from the modest exertion, the doctor gave me the result: 'you have angina'. Not really a surprise, after two months of experiencing moderate pain during short one-mile walks to work in the cold air, with syncope at the edges of my vision and a rather breathless five-minute rest needed on arrival. But still, I would rather have discovered that I was being a hypochondriac, or that these symptoms were a random after-effect of some virus.

I had to take another test, so I stepped outside the hospital during the enforced break. It was a beautiful sunny day. If this was Dante's 'dark wood', it was gleaming... but I felt lost nevertheless. Angina may not be very serious but the diagnosis felt like being told which bullet has my name on it. In a way my inner being had always felt solid, ongoing, but now it had become something else. Until today, like Norman MacCaig I might have said 'Self under self, a pile of selves I stand/Threaded on time' but (stumbling into the hospital's 'Applejack' cafe, with its surprisingly unhealthy sausage-themed menu) I felt like just one, scared little self. A small meat object with temporary self-consciousness and a long to-do list.

Route Projection

I am a downsman lost on friendly hills,
snagged in gorse and fretting:
how did I arrive, here,
in this exacting valley?

Maybe my map was wrong,
I missed some turn, the
lucky lightning stone lost
on a hurried contour.

Maybe the soft curves of the hard
chalk lead inevitably
here, to a place that was aways
mine. Soon strangers
will come, carry me over
stiles and fences of
an unwanted hill

and later my own hoped-for steps, flowing:
down past Thundersbarrow, Rest and be Thankful
and the Crooked Moon Hedge.

The sun finds the black branches.
It is still early. The paths are generous.

Southport

It could be summer if not for this
wind. Sun gleams on the curved
steel roofs of the Ocean Plaza
cinema where we once saw *Far From
Heaven*. Pleasureland has reopened
again and a ferris wheel turns at
the horizon, speck riders lifted
into a raked blue sky.

The tide here is long
and we seldom see water:
a jagged shell-line marks
the shore's true edge.

Diagnosis has slammed me
seriously into
this bright moment—
no meditation, no
mindful practice—
this hardwired spirituality
is just there, always-on.

Memo: keep this
crazy-edged bliss
surprised, dripping, open
once the waves recede
to the safe horizon.

Exploded

While I was remembering
exploded view diagrams

    motorcar, aeroplane, rocketship
    components spreading and frozen
    in pure space and bathed
    in rational light

outside the train window I saw
a suitcase lying broken on the bank

    shirts, tops and underwear
    slowly soaking and tumbled
    down to the gray margin
    abandoned from some furious moment

and thought:
how best to plot my heart

    valves, chambers and whispers
    marked-up, charted
    in an elusive interior:
            ghost-engine working.

Transactions

There was a guy swearing
an oath in the reception area:
the paperback Bible was curled
as if the solicitors thumbed through
Lamentations to Revelation
between appointments. He
had to pay five
pounds. Above the water
cooler was a framed poster
of Steve McQueen in *The Great*
Escape. I had called
in to hand over copies
of my passports and some bills, proving
self and its location, shoring up my
pre-op willmaking. Then

I went to the chain cafe where
Aisha (whom I once met at a party
and never know what to say) sold me low-
fat decaffeinated latte—I'm drinking
the absence of substances, atoning
for years of hidden arterial
silting. They had burlap-effect prints on the
wall: swirling beans and a casual-looking senior
man described as a 'coffee
maestro since 1976' which seemed
to me too short a period to make

a fuss about. Outside
it was market day on the market
street thanks to the market
Charter of 1286; I could buy fruit:
five pieces to place in the wailing
wall of health and maybe a small
rug with a rainbow unicorn
delineated in zesty pigment,
for hope. On maps

made before
motorways, red-artery roads
radiated from each market town,
a net across the common territory; these days I
hang in the cat's cradle woven
by hospitals clinics and surgeries, nothing
to offer back except sardonic quips and a
successful recovery: waiting
in stun and alarm I learn
to love imperfectly the imperfect
exchanges. Circling

the stalls, pigeons
scour the cobbles.

This poem written by Roy Anthony Bayfield
Chartered Marketer number 1117955
Costa Coffee Club cardholder 633780 93226 3000513 6

Blood, and thunder

For PW

I need a strong pulp
channel to deal with this
unwanted adventure:
stock the shelves with
yellow-edged paperbacks
pile up 25-cent
comic-books and
unleash the concrete poetry of
gunslingers
      sudden, hex and edge
sergeants
      rock and fury, or the
sword-and-planet men
        located in relation to
        mars, scorpio and the green star.

Send me out on a spree with a jaded
barbarian king; tomorrow I'll
buy a new dressing gown
some slippers and a
self-help book.

The Bypass Pilgrim doesn't quite live   in the workplace,
the homestead, the expected dreamlands
    all the screens go blank as his boots slowly fill with
blood
walking a strange High
    Street between
    appointments
    dislocated to the special hour
    populated with those who cannot quite
    make the necessary arrangements to
    keep their bodies indoors or keep
    thoughts inside their mouths—
    outside of clock-time
    it's all grey air and carrier bags,
    discount cigarettes
    and an endless muttering—
    the encyclopedia of unclear
    questions (unanswered)
    compiling itself on the common
    space between the bus station,
    the off-license, and the Coronation Park
plywood boxes covered with carpet, for displaying jewellery
    but without jewellery on them,
plastic trays with green plastic hedges shaped like parsley, for
displaying fish
    but without fish on them:
        so now make roadside shrines of these.

The placename 'Broadgreen' has an attractive ring to it—perhaps denoting an ancient wide common. These days Liverpool's Broadgreen is home to the hospital where, at the end of this month, I will be spending a few days having a cardiac bypass. A pilgrimage along re-routed arteries; a mashup heart created to get me back on the road. Culmination of six weeks since being diagnosed: an experience probably less stressful than a tour of duty in a warzone; probably more stressful than a season in a pantomime, with some of the characteristics of both. Maybe like unexpectedly finding oneself in the cast of a Mystery Play, in which the devils and angels keep changing places, the story seems familiar but doesn't make sense, and the stage maroons are armed with live ammo. Snowdrops and snowflakes delivering body blows in a winter that won't quit. Venous sabbatical.

I am happy enough to be booked in to Broadgreen. It is an excellent hospital by all accounts and an outpatient visit yesterday was as pleasant as such a thing could be. And the location interests me... way back in 2008 on the third leg of the walk (Maghull to Liverpool) I walked right past the hospital, on the Liverpool Loop, a deep disused railway cutting. So this pitstop is right next to the track itself. Comforting, like being wired up to my own personal leyline, connected to places and people that matter, north and south, past and future. Of course, back then I had no idea. At the time, I may not even have glanced in the direction of the hospital complex. So come all you ramblers, hear my tale—when you look into the darkness beyond the trees lining your route, consider that things dreadful and marvellous may lurk there. A future that will alter your heart.

I'll spend Holy Week in Broadgreen. This Lent I have given up many things, including 'peace of mind', though I'm not complaining. During this process I seem to have found my way back to reality—being here and doing things, rather than rushing on to next thing and worrying about the thing after that. There will be more to give up: the equipage for this trip is slim indeed.

Eventually, having parted with clothes, body-hair and consciousness (everything but my name tag), I'll be in the hands of the experts, fully surrendered...

Nothing left to do now but go through with it. And hope —that it works, that soon I'll be buoyed on a spring blood-tide, walking home.

2: TREATMENT

Within this space we cannot see.

Lectures on Subjects Connected with Clinical Medicine, Comprising Diseases of the Heart, Peter Mere Latham (1846)

Patient Journey

It was like a normal run out in the car
using roads that have started
holidays and led to parties,
graduations, shared meals.

This however was a special journey
leading to the Surgical Admissions Ward, Liverpool
Heart and Chest Hospital. We drove
without many words, past spring hedges and
Tudor-style semis and

inevitably, we arrived.

It was quiet this Palm Sunday,
like checking into a discreet hotel
with tamely brutal decor.
A nurse brought us sandwiches.
Wristbands with my birthday
in barcode form were
fitted to both arms.
My body hair was shaved.
A radio played 'Magic Weekend'
pop freighted with memories—
it was an odd time to be reminded
of love losing, lust crying,
eternal revolution.

A sign by the bed conveyed
patient care philosophy and details
of handwashing protocols but
all I saw were the largest of its printed words
fallen here from distant Buddhist
paperback titles

        Here

        Now.

This matter-of-fact
world of curtains and elbow taps
was not the place for an enormous
opera screaming wild emergency.
Feelings bled out pastel
in the routine-cooled
corporate space—soon

        (There

        Then   )

it would be time
for the next stage. Waiting we
said all we could think to say
for as long as we had time to say it.

White Gold Round

Entering this theatre involves
surrender
stripping down to essentials,
losing clothes,
identity, status, relationships and roles
keeping only wristband data, tattoos,
pre-existing scar tissue.

Leaving my wedding ring behind
was one of these necessary losses.

I remember buying it
one of a pair
Dublin 1993
there on my own, extending a work trip
hurrying down lyrically-famous streets with
lines from a Patrick Kavanagh poem in my head
(received via the Dubliners, via Van Morrison):
> 'On Grafton Street in November we tripped lightly
> along the ledge'
> (though the actual soundtrack at the time was a busker
> playing *American Pie*)
the rings found in a jewellers opposite Trinity College
plain bands with a knotwork pattern added by a calligrapher

resized back home in Wolverhampton in time for the wedding
when 'I gave her the secret sign'
and we passed through the circle—
17 years holding the endless pattern—
the first time we went out, on a blazing
Worcesterhire summer evening
an owl stood on a post, just yards away
holding us in its uncanny
rounding eyes.

Register

      I was
Admitted, and then variously, in part and at times repeatedly
Burped
Cannulated

Exercised
Fed
Grafted
Harvested
Infused
Jollied
Knapped
Labelled
Manhandled
Nebulised
Observed
Palpated
Questioned
Restarted
Shaved
Tagged
Undressed
Ventilated
Wired
X-rayed
Yrent, then
Zippered
         and finally
            Discharged.

        Meanwhile I
Ate
Breathed
Coughed
Desired
Expectorated
Forgot
Giggled
Hedged
Ideated
Joked
Kissed
Loafed
Mourned
Noted
Obeyed
Panicked
Queried
Refused
Sank
Tottered
Unspooled
Vowed
Whispered
X-marked the spot for future remembrance and
Yawed until I was triumphantly
                    Zeroed.

Bypass Pilgrim /2

No more route:

this is the destination.

> (Tons of blackened buttressed stone
> slamming into the earth and saints
> carved within saints carved within saints.)

To arrive at the place
of pilgrimage
is to arrive
at a super-definite
point,
so why be making
aimless circuits of the
cathedral square?

> (To which most people came in cars. A few in coaches.)

The pricing structures of menus and souvenirs
are not modulated to reward
a soggy map comprehensively
tramped through.

(Along the way: blinding headaches; sudden hysterical
friendships; inexplicable offense given and taken;
thoughts of work; dropped signals; blisters.)

The destination is briefly welcoming but then
it demands your next move.   So. Look sideways
at the shrines (at least one time) and start
the journey back.

Early on a Monday morning, carefree from the effects of the pre-med tablets and a hardcore psalm, I said 'see you in a bit' to Jennie (as it happens, the same words used at Heathrow in 1991 when she went to Russia for five months.) I was wheeled along the unhomely corridors to a small room adjacent to the operating theatre. Enjoying a brisk chat with the anaesthetist I lost consciousness, from the effects of what he had helpfully described as 'a controlled overdose of opiates'. I was allowed to sleep the clock round after the operation, so know nothing about a whole 24 hours. That being the case, with just a dim claim on a null day, I now hand over to Jen who was, thankfully, intensely present during that day and night:

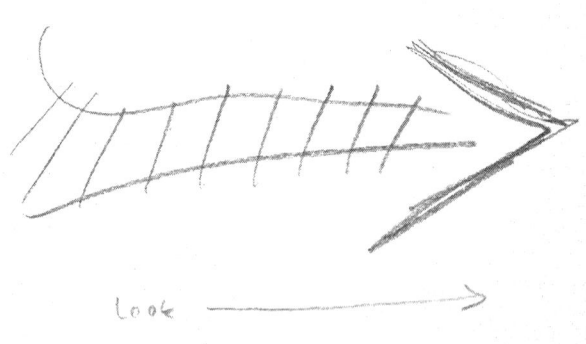

look ⟶

Telling the Bones
by Jennie Barnsley

Like my mother before me, I am an
independent bugger—bred
in the bone to
be myself
it never crossed my mind to
give away my name
til now
in this strange hour
I have become a stranger
"Mrs Bayfield?"

without demur
I answer to the stranger name
in this strange hour
I have become the rib I
disavowed for more than fifty years
scrimshawed out of
your cracked and wired cage

whatever I might have feared
this is not
dwindling
I grow
although it hurts
a stronger frame to
catch your
tottering old-man steps

while I was out

boundaries shifted
the flesh perimeter breached

in a campaign of intimate
devastation

kind violence
carried me
bodily
across unseen
frontiers and

meanwhile
miracles

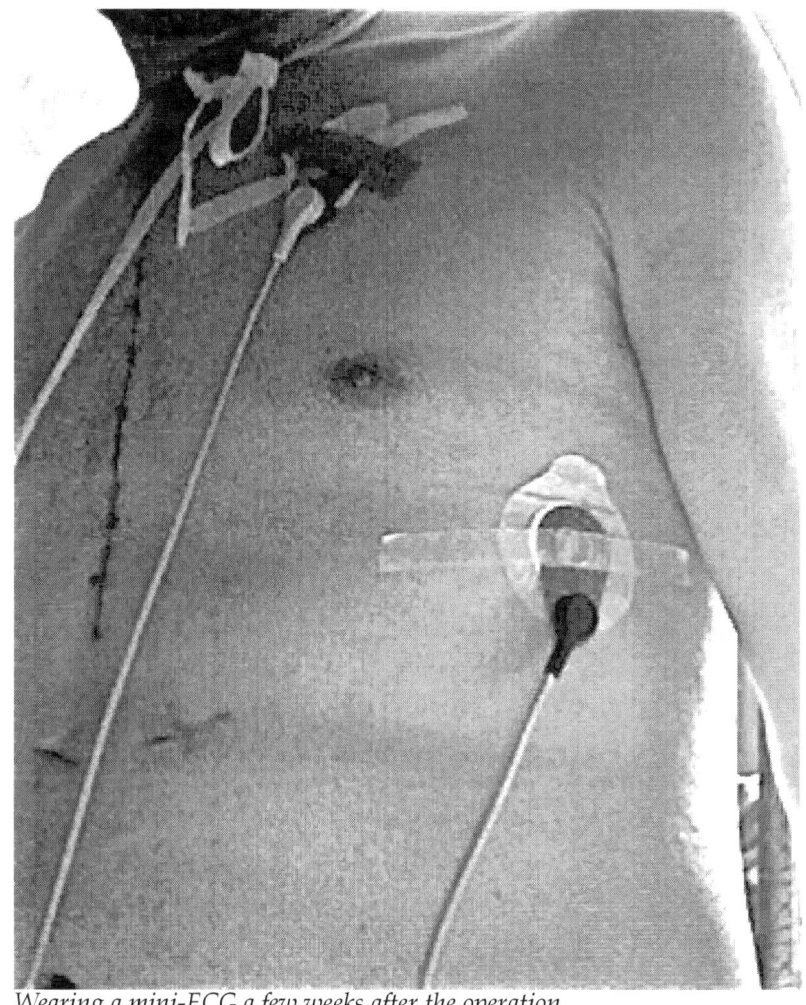

Wearing a mini-ECG a few weeks after the operation.

ICU

In the Intensive Care Unit I woke up
but did not cheer—
the intense bliss of living
was being held
in a future month
until I was ready.

                            Meanwhile
I was placid, underwater, drifting in
an antiseptic science fiction room,
sometimes watching men with intensely smooth faces
watching me, sometimes watching an older patient
who sat immobile like a ghost
waiting to be born. They gave me cornflakes,
and tea in a toddler's cup.

On the recovery ward I performed seven labours:
spoke with lucidity,
ate,
drank,
moved bowels,
walked the length of the corridor,
received medication,
understood instructions,
climbed one flight of stairs
and on Day 5 (Easter Saturday)
                          was rewarded with release
and on Day 73 (nothing special)

climbed a Pilgrim Way
to lean against the wind on 'the holiest
erthe in Englande'.
 The water-cuts
threaded the levels as I waited
by the tower for the blessing of
my second beat sequence and its
effective irrigation.
 They gave me an oat bar,
and red grail water in an old man's glass.

Cardiac Cowboy Saloon

Eight men in the high-dependency ward
busted in by a manly disease,
all old enough to remember
405-line TV flickering grey in long-ago
living rooms: *Bonanza, The Virginian,*
The High Chaparral.

We are feeble desperadoes
grizzled from the frontier
of bodies and time, caught
stumbling from the goldrush,
backshot, bad-luck cards dropping
to a sterile tavern
floor

a brief brotherhood, hide-out
gang in pajamas and white
pressure tights for whom
minor lavatorial triumphs
are cause for common celebration.

Plastic tubes dangle brightly,
like borrowed tribal jewellery.

Our scars prove us to be hard
men, but we are not at our best—

hair scrappy
steps hesitant
voices rusty.

Sometimes we whine.

But remember: there were times
when we looked better

    running across grass striped with sunlight
    posing tipsily for a wedding photo
    buying a sandwich at a service station
    forgetting

        to revel
        in our
        fragile power.

Found Text

"On the first or second day the nursing staff will ask you to sit out of bed and walk a short distance around the bed.

Day 2 following surgery — Walk 3 times to the Red heart. Do this twice today.

Day 3 following surgery — Walk 5 times to the Yellow heart. Do this twice today.

Day 4 following surgery — Walk 8 times to the Green heart. Do this twice today.

By the time you go home you should be walking freeing around the ward and the nurse or physiotherapy staff will ensure you can comfortably climb one flight of stairs."

<u>Note</u>

I walked the required number of times,
grateful for another hiking project.
The colour hearts were positioned offhand
among the notices of service-levels and advice
to eat oily fish. It is a typo
obviously but
I cheerfully accept
my commission to go

"walking
freeing"

(although I know where to walk but not
what to free.)

...

Christmas 1966 I spent in a
'Children's Unit' in Hove.
I remember the strangely deep baths,
the baffling rules, my dad
fixing the tree lights with tinfoil
during a visit, a card game with
lightning bolts as jokers, the ill and exiled
children singing *Silent Night*.

> I learned to be wary of these
> 'institutions'—
> the functional
> gardens, perpetually
> lit stairwells, poor
> food, notices
> and
> corridor-regimens that
> seem to say in adamant 'life
> is less amenable than you thought.'

Easter 2010 I spent in a
'Foundation Trust' in Liverpool.
I remember the ocean-bed ward floor,
the weakly-whispered phone calls,
a digital photo of a nearby city building
as decor, sheets of rain on flat roofs,
the pooled light nurse station

in the silence of the night.

A place of relentless skill and routine genius,
'the best heart hospital' everyone said, and I agree.

Even so I took a foil wrapper and made a tiny blade,
slept with one eye open,
ready for any
lightning.

3: REHABILITATION

"The blood is the life!"
Dracula, Bram Stoker (1897)

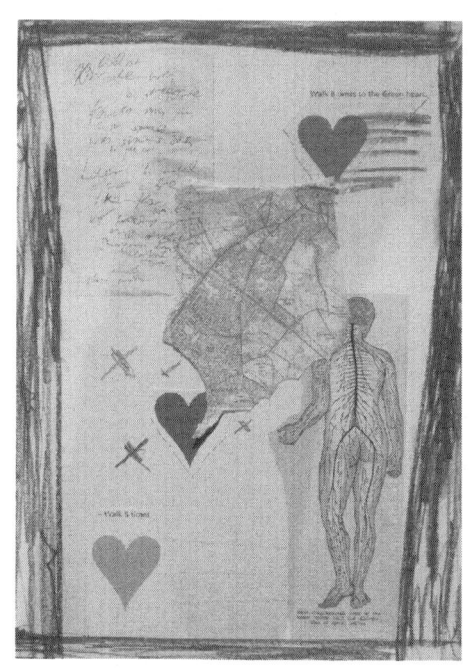

The Blue Sky Breeze Caresses Invisible Triggers

Waiting for the operation was a strange time. I tried to focus on the success and benefits, but the slim chance of failure and death was impossible to ignore. This is surely natural: imagine playing Russian roulette with, say, a dozen guns; all but one are completely empty so the odds are massively in your favour; still you ponder the one cold bullet.

People I love and hadn't seen enough of, sometimes for years, suddenly appeared. Some made detours to see me and sent gifts: lovely occurrences that nevertheless had an undercurrent of poignancy. I felt like the passing hero being fêted on the way to the long barrow, clapped on the shoulder for the last time and given a disc of rare Scott Walker tracks with which to pay the ferryman.

But this wasn't that kind of story. I am home now, wounded more than departed, sitting

—with spring sunshine warming one side of my face,

—with the realisation that the statistics have been tamed but not erased.

I look into the garden: the thornbush punches, say, ten thousand white blossoms into the sky.

There is no more need to play Russian roulette—the guns are everywhere now.

Side FX

He left three bop pills for ten, two and four
And man when they hit me, I landed in the middle of the floor.
- Bop Pills (Skipper - McNatt) Macy 'Skip' Skipper (Sun, recorded 1956)

On a lifelong prescription for
blockers and thinners
inhibitors and antagonists, daily I
stake coloured flags into an invisible
battleground.

There may be 'uncommon
side effects'—dizziness,
confusion, hearing
disturbances: dropping
      into a whorl made of caper-
      movies, ballgowns on balconies, champagne falling;
      dreams of lostness and unending travel;
      wanting silences
      filled with forgotten
      songs. I took one puff
            of dynamite
            and strode across the snow;
            I took two puffs of dynamite
            and fell down on the ground
            —woke up lying on another
            man's coat.

The chemical lozenges are counters
in a game where winning the statistics
may delay losing the whole campaign,
for an unspecified period,
depending on individual conditions.

Meanwhile my beta-blocked heart
pumps willow-thinned blood
                              lizard-slow
as I weigh odds like a gambler—
which harm to choose
over which danger, a scruple
of oil to a pennyweight of
flesh, and the product added
to a pound of luck.

No Sleep 'til Ragnarok

The white god guards the rainbow
bridge, unsleeping, scanning for detail
—the growth of plants, the movements of armies.
From his sky-mountain hall he peers
at the end of the world.

In the bent stick hours he hears
my heartbeat. Companionably, we look
out into the predawn clouds,
standing watch
for the collapse
of pensions, the death
of bees, some further
occlusion of bodily channels.

One day he will blow the calling-horn to awaken all
the gods to battle.

Today I will breathe
into the angle of your neck
until you stir.

Bloods

Our bloods pulse a thousand
languages within the slowly-falling
towers of our bodies as we
    wait—

    waiting starts with taking a number
on any weekday except
for the morning when they do the
Warfarin clinic.

If you arrive early and take the first
number you have to wait
until the phlebotomist gets there.
If you arrive later people will have taken numbers and be
queuing already
and you will have to wait. Either way I bring a book and

    read

"[his] heart beat faster...[and] the air smelt of blood...[which]
glistened/spilling/dribbled...[it was a] bloody mess...[but]
you got you let anyone ride his own trail and dodge his own
bullets...his heart ached...I'll make him cry blood"

    avoiding reading
  news

    where gunfire makes wounds worse than mine

in distant places, in neighbouring counties

towers fall in our disputed
heartlands, someone's always
climbing from the wreckage
leaving bloody handprints

red fingers typing
into the networks everywhere
messages we sometimes
           hear

fractured, preoccupied, waiting.

The test results are filed.

"[He sang] *Weep all ye little rains*."

Desire Paths

I wanted to rewalk my origin story
kicking up chalk dust on gorse hills
to the Devil's Dyke via Skeleton Hovel,
an everyday trip from my mum's house but
impractical from 300 miles away with wired
sternum and sutures healing. Instead it's

rehab walks in a three-mile radius
to the Devil's Wall and Seldom Pond,
tracing routes never bothered with before and
surprised to find the gorse hills
right here, after all. In some secret movement

my flesh and bone has knitted them into place
yellowhammer, hawthorn, queen anne's lace.

Charms

       Filling time during enforced
       rehab leisure, in gift
       shops galleries and retail parks,
       where the shelves and walls are
       punctuated with
...hearts made of chocolate
...hearts made of mirror
...hearts made of cotton
...hearts made of twigs
...hearts made of mother of pearl
...hearts made of projected light
...hearts made of pixels
...hearts made of paper
...hearts made of wax
...hearts made of wire
...hearts made of felt
...hearts made of alloys, or silver, or plated with gold
...hearts made of leather
...hearts sequinned, studded with buttons, supporting clock
hands or metal butterflies or printed with

                 further hearts

hearts
formed,
transported, delivered, placed out in view

hearts made of warning, like
dead predators

hearts made of incantation, like
prayer flags

hearts made of naming, like
directory signs:

hearts at work on the perimeter fence

    hearts to bake cakes,
    hold mementos
    or
    leave written
    messages.

...

The world's apparent heart
has been a verb
since 1975:
'I ♥
NY'
the famous
trademark rebus
forged in American
Typewriter

Meanwhile my
UK ♥
is just
a secret interior hearth-god

devoid of grand claims but
delivering sporadic blessings

I ♥ a raptor hovering over a motorway verge
I ♥ a dog rose growing on a security fence
I ♥ horses running beneath the flyover,
        river shining

Recovery

At night we hear
owls.

At the start I walked
five minutes
twice a day,
climbed stairs
three times,
watched TV for
a hundred
hours, living placebo
lives
on Atlantis,
on a patrol
boat, in some small
American towns.
I saw my scars in the mirror and
blinked.

Our first day-trip was to
a supermarket where
I drank tea poured
from a pot
that I could not carry
while you did shopping I could not
help with
and we left by a door I could not

open.
It was as invigorating as a day
on Striding Edge.

One day I sat
on the floor and realised
I could not stand up. You
pulled me to vertical and we
looked
at each other
surprised
as if we had
met there
by accident.

At night I hear
a giant heartbeat.

I played patience games,
grew out my cropped hair,
learned to like jazz,
read Sexton Blake and
Sappho and
looked at the heart-help books
with pictures of smiling
pensioners on bikes and
holiday beaches,

and recipes for
low-fat meals.

I learned to uncross my legs,
remembered to cough despite the pain,
drank green tea and multiple
juices. The scar on my arm described
a shallow S and we remembered
when the dressing came off and the bruises
looked like tiger stripes. We became hypervigilant
for symptoms but also for the physical
geography of the ground
of our being.

Later we walked
good miles
by the sparrow hedge and the owls'
shed. My scars mulched down.
The damage sank.

At night you hear
scrawling.

Diet sheet

1

Don't tempt me towards
the grave with your 'Naughty
but nice death by chocolate'—
I'm busy walking the health
apocalypse from Alpha-linolenic
acid to Omega-3
and there's no time for dessert.

2

Rumours of scientific treatises
arrive daily in the rehab garden.
Cooling down from aerobic steps
amongst the statues and bolted
container plants we read of new
permissions and revised prohibitions.

3

Archaeo-pathological analysis of my
arterial silt revealed relics
of conviviality, boredom,
pragmatism and bohemian interludes
secreted in the strata.

4

Silver shoals of sardines
are now marked
for death to feed
my healthy maw.

5

'Skin is the enemy'
said the nurse, referring
mainly to chicken.

6

'Avoid Eating'
the visible, the excess, that of unknown origin.

7

Enjoy your meal.

Dwelling-Place

I became forgetful of hearts
but when you turned
your tapestry round
the shadows formed the familiar
curves, Cupid's atria—

considering
        palpitations and the patency of grafts
                —is this how it feels, getting mortal?

recovering
        capability and the routines of exchange
                —is this how it feels, getting grown-up?

surrendering
        heartfulness into the ground of the world
                —is this how it feels, getting human?

        in the Taj Mahal, camera
        flashes from the next table
        making indoor summer lightning

        a woman in a grey suit striding
        alone up Bridport South Street,
        holding a half-done drink in a plastic
        glass lit by the 9.20 midsummer sunset,

her face a cold flame

precession of equinoxes

delineating the nature of this sequence
of moments: *'the Long-Desired...nearer
than my own heart's eager blood / Yet further
from me than the dimmest star'*; stars held
in the 3am sky like snowflakes

waiting to fall

and to fall

Othona, Burton Bradstock, June 2010
Title and quoted matter from *The Trysting Place*, A.M. Curtis, 1913

Clock Tower

We walked into town
for cardiac rehab
and a nice lunch.

There was an old lady

lying at the foot of the
clock tower
paramedics and gawpers
attending.

Red liquid ran
between the cobbles—
broken out of a shopping
bottle, headwound
or sheered aortic valve and
rilled into a pattern
of wings

red birds spelling
a new sentence
for the time-owned sky.

Comic Interlude

I wasn't snarling unsayable
complaints I was
laughing it off,
calling it plumbing,
referring to bionic powers and
a baboon heart.

My scars were on the Internet
for general amusement, wounds
accompanied with an assortment
of hats and costumes, a promise to reappear
as the Tin
Woodman.

Beneath it all a darker
wit drew me down.
I held the line with the black gang.

Ready for the smart
comeback.

Cardiac 2.0

only plays music
never heard before

only saves pictures
taken today

needs new passwords

time for watching
> paths slowly appearing in a
> sapling wood, whilst parsing code to
> spray language through multiple
> devices

> tapping the human kaleidoscope
> where someone is going for sushi, everyone
> seems drunk tonight, oil soaks the delta,
> someone is lost on their way home,
> the living and dead are deported,
> vespers is starting in the virtual abbey,
> someone cannot sleep, weeds
> grow through the rusting hulks
> of Russian locomotives,
> and there's an empty new-built village
> surrounded by desert
> and a blizzard of messages

Writing Instruments

My dad carries a fountain pen older than me,
while I leave boxes of 20, 50 or 100 disposable biros
in every room. Both of us always want to reach out
and find something with which to write.

His circuit diagrams and music staves.
My outlines and ellipses.

§

Arteries are the diameter of
biro refills
catheters are the thickness of
pencil leads:
the talk (with slides) explained the mechanics
of the things that had already gone (irrevocably) wrong and
the treatments already undertaken (bringing us
to this room)—as if we were
shadow paramedics training to go back
in time to rewrite
our pulse-fisted fates

§

come write me down

The 'Health Work and Well-Being' building

On the path from the car park
there was a heart-shaped pendant
jammed in a crack between
paving stones.

Inside, the walls were the colour of
pistachio ice cream—a pale
Emerald City with National Health
pop radio: Dusty Springfield, her heart
landing in the middle of nowhere.

The doctor said
'soon'
I could
'phase back in'
to working weeks—
the same dispensation
offered to returners
from maternity,
though I haven't given
birth to anything
unless it is a
(provisional,
deferred)
sketch of
a dissolving into some
shared   dissolving.

C.A.B.G.

"He's had cabbage" I heard
the nurse say
but she did not mean Sweetheart, Savoy
or January King but
> Coronary
> Artery
> Bypass
> Graft
the proper name for the surgery
that had me lying in a doctor's round.

Spoken into "cabbage"
it almost seems homely.
Even in full the words are mostly tame:
"graft" a name for a shovel and a ditch and
something done with plants and wool,
arterial "bypasses" safely in roadmaps;
but "coronary" brings dubious
splendours—crowns, lights in the sky,
dusty wreaths.

Away from doctors we weave
new things from the wreck:
walk the escarpment, make stews,
cultivate vegetables.

Soon there could be actual cabbages—
Sojourner, Clarity, Leap-year's Knight.

Outpatient Appointment

Bud Abbott: *Get up on your feet. It's only a dummy.*
Lou Costello: *Dummy nothin'. It was smart enough to scare me.*
Abbott and Costello Meet Frankenstein, Universal International Pictures
(1948)

The waiting room was filled with
golems,
tulpas,
automata:
our stand-ins.
None of us had been brave
enough to come in person,
at least not in
full.

The doctor showed an X-ray movie of
the pre-op heart in black and white,
my own Universal horror,
veins kinked like winter branches
under moon-stricken
Carpathian clouds.

She told me the procedure had been
'on-pump',

my heart
stopped
my brain
kept alive
by machines;
'depending on your philosophy
you were dead
for those hours'
but not anymore so
now I could be
discharged.

The corridors were filled
with
werewolves,
vampires,
revenants:
all of us content enough
with how strange life was
rigged.

Bypass Pilgrim /3

The Bypass Pilgrim
walks some hard miles
to avoid the silted ruins,
holds his healing wound
like a healing relic.

There is map legend—
contours? boundary-paths?—
etched on his limbs

the scar on his chest
looks like an arrow, looks
like a compass needle.

heart of gold, beaten thin
      breastplate translucent and scarred
            he aches
                 towards

                 a complicated city
                 shuddering rhythmically into being,

            a single breath
on a green track.

Release

after two billion
beats your heart

stopped//

restarted, the
second beat sequence
pulsing on
a new shore

—so—

//check
the horizon,
find some good
water

then

go

The last entry in my walking journal, before diagnosis stopped the walk for a while, was written after hiking from Chalfont St Giles to Langley in Berkshire, with Paradise Lost as a companion. It concluded with this piece of predictive text:

> Another mile of wood and wintry sunshine, some muddy paths to the station, and the day's walk was finished. Elsewhere, the rain I had enjoyed was washing bridges away, flooding homes. There were autumn leaves still unfallen on the branches, and also some spring green come unnaturally early; in a couple of weeks I would be 48, a year-and-a-day left to reach the 50th year where the endpoint of this journey should lie; a bit more time 'treading the crude consistence' of ill-defined territory, 'bog or steep...strait, rough, dense, or rare'; pointing lenses into the sun, metastasising words and pixels and unfolding fresh maps.

Back now to walk on from Langley I have a battered paperback in my rucksack (*Trap Angel!* Sphere, 1973), a Venus HB pencil and a notebook. The last walk was solitary, but now we're walking together, over aquaducts, past half-hidden meadows and the backs of factories and haulage yards where men take breaks on broken chairs placed by the water.

Before this walk was broken, the paint on the narrowboats was slightly brighter, less weed drifted in the canal water, the brick field was a building, the steel frame a volume of space in air.

If I mattered overmuch these changes would be calibrated to contain my absence, and the St George flags on the canalside apartments would celebrate my dragon being slain. But I matter just enough, so we just walked, sunshine and dragonflies.

And the next day I was given a holly staff.

Southwick Hill Tunnel /
A27 Shoreham Bypass

You might expect this hill to be dead,
run through with carriageways,
its insides hollow, rendered
endlessly open through the application
of innovative Tunnelling Methods

congestion-relief traffic
speeding through slow millions
of chalk years hidden.

Drivers glancing up at
where the hill curves in shadow
over the white tunnel-sockets
see the lines made by ancient droving,
recent dog exercise, rights of way
and small figures, moving

including me, walking and rewalking
the tract I claim as the key text   (my AutoBioGeography)
looking for the border of nature   (any new cut into the chalk)
overlooking the bypass valley   (some kind of SuperNature)
and what was all this death stuff
anyway.

...in the Sky!'

in the exercise class we lift
our assorted shirts to fit the heart
monitors

some of us bear the threefold
sigil of the bypass
—one upright over two
obliques

some of us are in everyday
shirts with collars while
others approximate
gym or sports gear

my worn t-shirt has a picture of
the Justice League—a gathering of perfected
bodies, ardent to force definite Effects
from the sublime Causes that run bright
through their musculature, their eyes

got my first comic when I was
ten—*Peril of the Paired Planets*
gave them up last
year—*Final Crisis*

after Superman's music of the spheres sang
death's grey god away

there was nothing much left to see—and
anyway I now have my own chest emblem
and, relatively speaking, super powers

breathing more oxygen
growing new capillaries

seeing with ArtVision
even here, slogging circuits in a tiny gym
with a felt-pen Green Heart spreading
through my namebadge

still listening for the
call

'Look, Up...

Quintessence

The five of hearts is really the five
of cups, the card of disappointment
—petals ripped by fiery winds, a dark figure by the river,
turning away from a lost bridge

and I have five bypass grafts, bright
loops bringing oxygen and, thereby, some strange
jouissance into my valves and chambers

while in corridors and classrooms I quip
about having 'five hearts'

and the educational talks for cardiac patients covered
exercise, diet, relaxation, sex and sundry other
pages from the picturebooks
each of us was choosing for future time

so I walked up the Street of a Thousand Restaurants, where
lifesize photos of attractive catering interiors had been pasted
over the windows of several real but currently closed
establishments—perfumes smell different on older skin, due
in part to the action of fatty acids and lipid peroxides—but the
salt sea air whipped in anyway

and it had been a short journey
from near-ultimate nakedness
(spatchcocked on an operating table)
to choosing a five-day week's shirts and ties
(wondering at the utility of strips of coloured cloth)

and the fifth dimension is

      imagination

and the fifth element is

      æther

      so I was asleep

along the river, asleep
across the bridge

dreamed enough details
to make a journey back

NOTES

Broken hearted I will wander
The quote from Norman MacCaig is from his poem *Summer Farm*, which can be found in *The Poems of Norman MacCaig* (Polygon, 2005). I was introduced to this and thereby to MacCaig's work, among many good things, by 'Solitary Walker' on his blog <http://solitary-walker.blogspot.com/>

Route Projection
The placenames used are all real and can be found at TQ2208 and 2307. Detailed scrutiny may lead the geographically-informed reader to comment along the lines of 'Hang on, you say you're walking to Brighton, which is *East* Sussex, but these places are clearly in the West—if you went that way, you'd be heading to Southwick.' This is true and my actual walk will probably be on more prosaically-titled East Sussex paths. However I could not resist the names. Perhaps, just as the Devil has all the best tunes, West Sussex has all the best placenames.

Transactions
Thanks to Aisha for agreeing to appear in this poem. And to Jenni for making the necessary arrangements—an unprecedented masterpiece in the field of human communication.

Blood, and Thunder
It may well be that only the dedicatee will immediately decode the cultural references. The works of Oliver Strange, 'Frederick H. Christian', 'George G. Gilman', Edgar Rice Burroughs, 'Alan Burt Akers' and Lin Carter, as well as the war and western comics produced by DC and Marvel will reward the curious. If a 'spree with a jaded / barbarian king' appeals to you as much it does to me, you will find that *Conan the King* 28 (Marvel, 1985) contains a marvelously wistful evocation of middle-age, the weight of responsibility and the poignancy of lost years. And a guest appearance by Red Sonja.

Patient Journey
...'Buddhist paperbacks' such as *Be Here Now* by Ram Dass (Crown, 1971).

Register
'Yrent' is almost cheating, I know. It's in Chaucer and Spenser, and it can be used in Scrabble. In our household we pronounce it 'eye-rent' and use it to mean 'rent' as in 'torn'. Please help to rehabilitate this word.

No Sleep 'Til Ragnarok
Heimdall is the 'white god', 'bent stick' co-star of the poem. I first encountered him in *Myths of the Norsemen* by Roger Lancelyn Green, and soon afterwards in the *Mighty Thor* comics of Stan Lee and Jack Kirby (*Journey into Mystery* 83 et seq, Marvel.) The 'No Sleep 'Til...' formulation comes from the title of the Motörhead live album *No Sleep 'Til Hammersmith*.

Southwick Hill Tunnel
The 'innovative' construction technique used was the New Austrian Tunneling Method.

...in the Sky'
The *Peril of the Paired Planets* story (by Denny O'Neill) was in Justice League of America #82 (DC 1970) while *Final Crisis* was a series originally published in 2008, again by DC. 'Peril...' was an early example of a story where the superheroes encounter versions of themselves from alternate worlds; 'Final Crisis', written by Grant Morrison, was the latest expression of what has become a subgenre based on this trope.

Apparently exercise does cause new capillaries to grow —a process called 'angiogenesis'. Isn't that just lovely?

THANKS

Thanks are due to many people, including

—Friends, family and colleagues who have supported me in ways too numerous to mention.

—The clinicians, nurses, physiotherapists, General Practitioners and other professionals who have helped to improve my cardiac health, particularly the Consultant Cardiac Surgeon and her team, who sliced, diced and reassembled me.

—People who have encouraged me in my writing, including John Channing, Rhiannon Evans, Dave Finchett, Mari Hughes-Edwards, Helen Pearson, Claire Penketh, Robert Sheppard, Ian Smith, Andre Stitt and Roy Smiles ('Just write, you mook') who also provided the Scott Walker compilation mentioned in *The Blue Sky Breeze...*'

—John Channing again, for providing the rest of the soundtrack to my recuperation, and the rest of the Piccadilly Cowboys, for keeping me sane.

—Another John, John Holding, for making the holly staff that will support me on the remainder of the pilgrimage; and to Rick for constructing its fantastic ferrule.

—Colleagues at Edge Hill University who provided incalculable support, including the amazing people in my team who ran a busy communications department while I spent three months watching TV, strolling the hills and writing this.

—The Othona Community at Burton Bradstock, for giving me some place to go.

—Susan Sanford for inspiration and collage materials.

—Ursula, for holding my outline.

—Contributors to the hearts2hearts forum <http://www.heart2hearts.co.uk/> who did so much to reduce my fears to manageable proportions.

—And Jennie, for punctuation, grammar, all that stuff and pretty much everything else.

So thanks everyone—this book is offered as a tiny return gift.

ABOUT THE AUTHOR

Roy Bayfield has written and performed his work over the past three decades, lurking at the thresholds of various subcultures.

His story *Signal* appeared in the anthology *Britpulp! New Fast and Furious Stories from the Literary Underground* (Tony White, ed., Sceptre, 1997) and he has written for various small press publications.

His blog *Walking Home to 50* has a dedicated following, and the post *Destination: Argleton!* led to international exposure and appearances on national radio and TV. His academic and professional writing ranges across social media, marketing, fantasy fiction and film adaptation.

He lives near Liverpool, with his partner Jennie Barnsley, where he works as Director of Corporate Communications for Edge Hill University.